Q&A: Life's Mysteries Solved!

WHY DO CARS NEED GAS?

And Other FAQs About Machines

By Amy Hayes

Gareth Stevens PUBLISHING

Please visit our website, www.garethstevens.com. For a free color catalog of all our high-quality books, call toll free 1-800-542-2595 or fax 1-877-542-2596.

Cataloging-in-Publication Data

Names: Hayes, Amy.
Title: Why do cars need gas? / Amy Hayes.
Description: New York : Gareth Stevens Publishing, 2017. | Series: Q & A: life's mysteries solved!| Includes index.
Identifiers: ISBN 9781482447736 (pbk.) | ISBN 9781482447750 (library bound) | ISBN 9781482447743 (6 pack)
Subjects: LCSH: Motor vehicles–Miscellanea–Juvenile literature. | Transportation–Miscellanea–Juvenile literature. | Aeronautics–Miscellanea–Juvenile literature. | Machinery–Juvenile literature.
Classification: LCC TL547.H39 2017 | DDC 629.04–dc23

Published in 2017 by
Gareth Stevens Publishing
111 East 14th Street, Suite 349
New York, NY 10003

Designer: Andrea Davison-Bartolotta
Editor: Kristen Nelson

Photo credits: Cover, p. 1 (car) Teddy Leung/Shutterstock.com; cover, p. 1 (gas pump) advent/ Shutterstock.com; p. 4 Anastasiya Maksymenko/Hemera/Thinkstock; p. 5 (main) JuliusKielaitis/Shutterstock.com; p. 5 (inset) Miles Willis/Getty Images News/Getty Images; p. 6 Frank Wasserfuehrer/Shutterstock.com; p. 7 (top) Mike Focus/Shutterstock.com; p. 7 (bottom) Olaf Schulz/Shutterstock.com; p. 8 fotohunter/Shutterstock.com; p. 9 JTB/Universal Images Group/Getty Images; p. 10 (doodle) Aleks Melnik/Shutterstock.com; p. 10 (main) Dusan Zidar/Shutterstock.com; p. 11 Robert Niedring/MITO Images/Getty Images; p. 12 HeroImages/Getty Images; p. 13 (screw) Kucher Serhii/Shutterstock.com; p. 13 (wedge) Petr Salinger/Shutterstock.com; p. 13 (inclined plane) Grandpa/Shutterstock.com; p. 13 (pulley) guillermo_bass/Shutterstock.com; p. 13 (lever) Stephen VanHorn/Shutterstock.com; p. 13 (wheel) tatui suwat/Shutterstock.com; p. 14 Monkey Business Images/ Shutterstock.com; p. 15 Time & Life Pictures/The LIFE Images Collection/Getty Images; p. 16 Bacho/ Shutterstock.com; p. 17 (main) VannPhotography/Shutterstock.com; p. 17 (inset) Bloomberg/Getty Images; p. 18 (icicles) Kamenuka/Shutterstock.com; p. 18 (main) Fuse/Corbis/Getty Images; pp. 19, 27 (inset) Dorling Kindersley/Thinkstock; p. 20 wavebreakmedia/Shutterstock.com; p. 21 JGI/Jamie Grill/Getty Images; p. 22 Tropical Press Agency/Stringer/Hulton Archive/Getty Images; p. 23 Comstock Images/Getty Images; p. 24 Paul Brennan/Shutterstock.com; p. 25 Xavier Pironet/Shutterstock.com; p. 26 (inset) Jack Hollingsworth/Getty Images; pp. 26–27 hxdbzxy/Shutterstock.com; p. 28 (top) Encyclopedia Britannica/UIG/Getty Images; p. 28 (bottom) courtesy of Wikimedia Commons; p. 29 Mimadeo/Shutterstock.com.

Printed in the United States of America

CPSIA compliance information: Batch #CS16GS: For further information contact Gareth Stevens, New York, New York at 1-800-542-2595.

Contents

Words in the glossary appear in **bold** type the first time they are used in the text.

Get Moving!

Mighty Machines

Every part of our lives is affected by the fantastic machines around us. From lamps to cars to roller coasters, machines make all sorts of wonderful things possible. But how do these machines work, and how are they powered? These questions and more will be answered in this book!

Q: Why do cars need gas?

A: Cars use gasoline to power their engine. Car engines need a lot of energy to move from place to place. The energy is created in an engine by **combustion**. Gas is an important part of this combustion. It mixes with air, the two are put under a lot of pressure, and then a spark causes a tiny explosion! The energy created from lots of tiny controlled explosions moves the car.

Right now, most cars need gas. But electric cars don't! They're powered by a rechargeable **battery**. More cars that run without gas may exist in the future.

inSIDe Explosions

Car engines are called internal combustion engines because combustion happens inside the engine.

Q: How do planes fly?

A: Planes are very heavy, so it seems strange they can fly above the clouds. However, planes use **physics** to help them beat gravity and **drag**. Planes use two forces: lift and thrust. Lift is the force that pushes the plane up. It's created by the shape of the airplane's huge wings, which make the air flowing over the wings move faster than the air flowing under the wings. When air moves faster, its pressure becomes lower. The difference in pressure above and below the wing creates lift. The engines of the airplane create thrust, which moves the plane forward very fast. When thrust and lift become more powerful than gravity and drag, the airplane rises. In fact, air moves around the plane and pushes the plane up!

Get That DRAG

When airplanes have to come down, the wings use flaps that increase drag, which slows the airplane. This helps a plane come down smoothly.

Q: Why do trains need tracks?

A: Trains need tracks to guide them on their way. Tracks lessen **friction**, so trains run smoothly and quickly across the tracks! Some trains are electric, and their tracks have a third rail that provides all the electricity that powers the train!

The Space Between

The distance between the two tracks of a train track is called the gauge. The gauge of the track is extremely important. If you don't have the right gauge, your train can't go on the track!

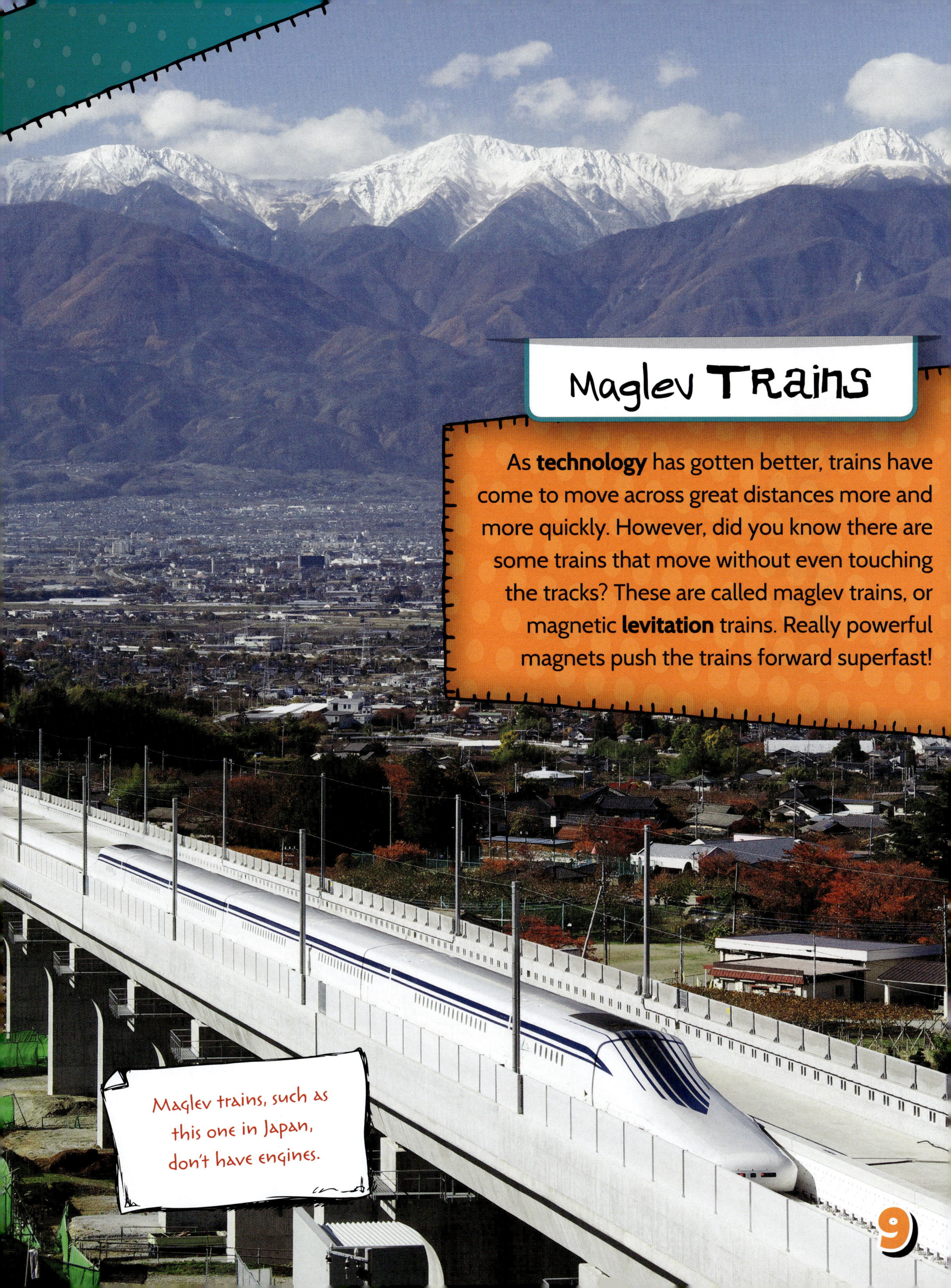

Maglev Trains

As **technology** has gotten better, trains have come to move across great distances more and more quickly. However, did you know there are some trains that move without even touching the tracks? These are called maglev trains, or magnetic **levitation** trains. Really powerful magnets push the trains forward superfast!

Maglev trains, such as this one in Japan, don't have engines.

POWERED BY PEOPLE

Q: What do bike gears do?

A: Gears are toothed wheels. They're a type of machine that helps move energy from one place to another. On a bike, gears connected by a chain help move the energy created by pedaling to the wheels.

The gears and chain on a bicycle help create a human-powered machine!

Fast and Slow, UP and Down

Bike gears help change the amount of energy you need to push your bike forward. If you're riding across a flat surface and you want to go faster, you can switch to a higher gear, making pedaling harder, but allowing you to move faster. If you get to the bottom of a steep hill and need more energy to go up it, you can switch into a lower gear. Though you'll move more slowly, it will be easier to get up the hill.

Q: How do skateboards turn?

A: It might seem as though skateboards would have trouble turning—aren't skateboards just wheels and a board? But if you've ever been on a skateboard, you know how easily it moves depending on which way you lean. This is because every skateboard has trucks. Trucks have metal **axles** that connect the wheels of the skateboard to the deck, or the board you stand on. Trucks have long, flat axles in the shape of a T. As the wheels roll, the trucks control where the axles will go. Your feet on the deck provide pressure, turning the direction of the axles.

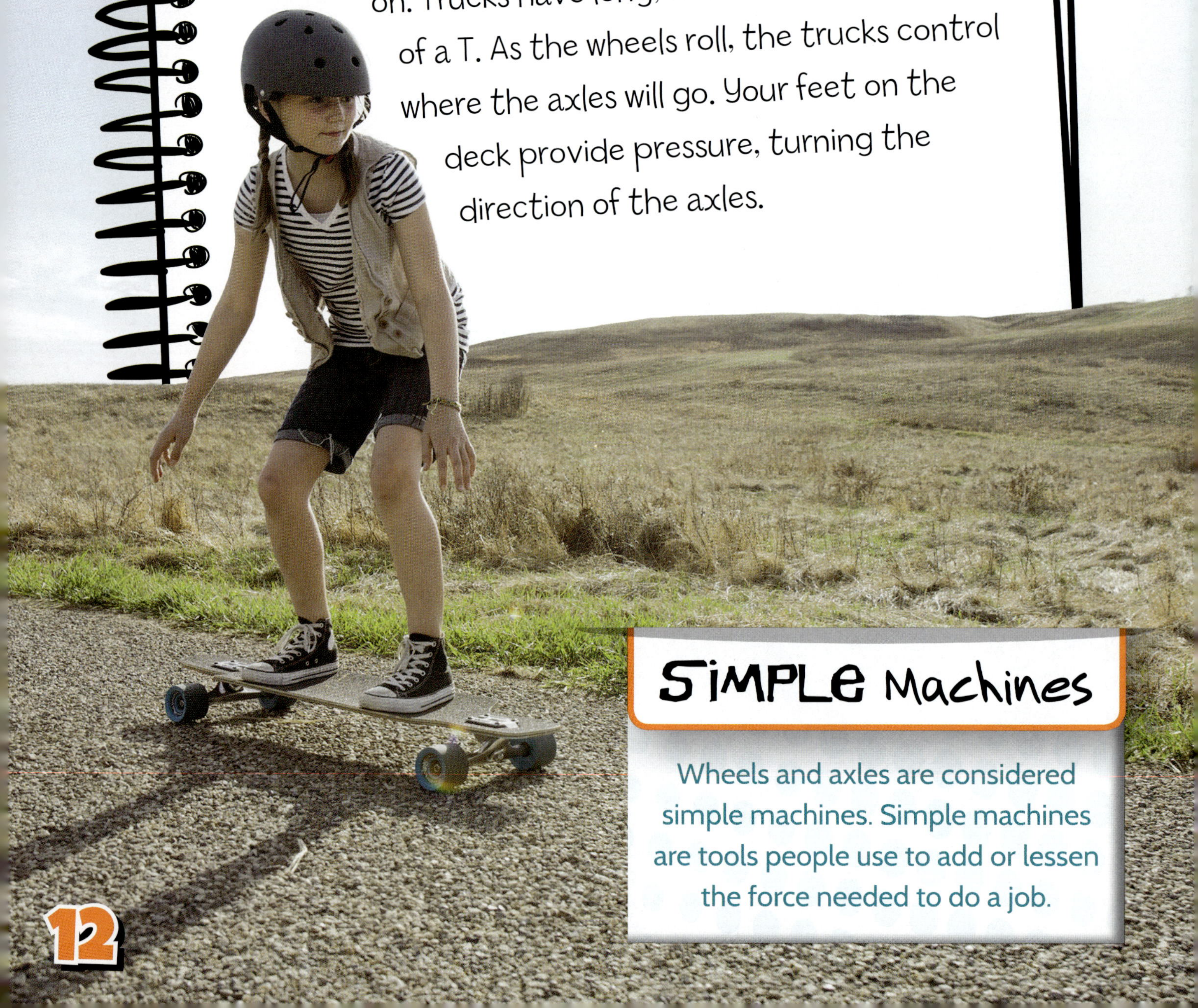

SIMPLE Machines

Wheels and axles are considered simple machines. Simple machines are tools people use to add or lessen the force needed to do a job.

Simple Machines

wheel and axle:
a wheel can help you roll something with less friction; an axle connects the wheel to what's being moved

lever:
anything that can **pivot** or move something back and forth

pulley:
a wheel and axle with a rope or chain attached; allows you to lift heavy things because it works with gravity to move something

inclined plane:
a slope that makes moving something up easier

screw:
an inclined plane wrapped around a pole that holds things together

wedge:
a sideways inclined plane that helps push things apart

TECH QUESTIONS

Q: Can computers think?

A: Computers are a type of machine that executes **complex** math very quickly. They can answer many questions that might force a person to think very hard. However, computers can't think for themselves. They're machines that are programmed to do a series of tasks, but it takes a person to create the program for the computers to use. This's why they are called computers—they don't think, they compute! "To compute" means "to calculate," or work through a series of math operations, such as addition, subtraction, and multiplication.

Computer ATTACK!

Many science fiction stories are based upon the idea that at some point in the future, computers will become **conscious**. In most of these stories, thinking computers end up fighting humans!

The First Computer

The first electronic computer was built at the University of Pennsylvania and completed in 1946. It was called ENIAC, which stood for **E**lectronic **N**umerical **I**ntegrator **a**nd **C**omputer.

The first computers were very large. ENIAC filled a whole room!

Q: Why do phones need to be charged?

A: Cell phone fun ends when that little battery symbol gets red and the phone dies. Phones die when the battery in them no longer has any charge left. Cell phones use lithium-ion batteries, which are small, light batteries that can store energy for many hours. However, lithium-ion batteries need to be recharged.

Reversible Reactions

In lithium-ion and other rechargeable batteries, the chemical reaction that releases the electricity can be reversed. This means energy can be put back into the battery, and you can use it again. However, this only works for a while. Even some of the best lithium-ion batteries only last 2 to 3 years.

People are working on many different ways to make batteries last longer.

Out of Juice

Regular batteries work by creating a chemical reaction that releases energy over time, but also **depletes** the battery—which means it doesn't work forever. Imagine if you had to buy a new battery every time your phone lost its charge!

Q: How do refrigerators stay cold?

A: It might sound strange, but though you can feel cold when you open a fridge door, cold doesn't technically exist. Instead, it's just the absence, or lack, of heat! Heat is a type of energy. So what's happening is that this energy is being removed from the air in your fridge.

Evaporation and Heat

When liquids **evaporate**, they take heat energy from the area around them. It's the same reason you might feel chilly after getting out of a pool, even on a hot day–the water on your skin takes some of your heat away as it evaporates!

Fridges have a special type of **coolant** that runs through **coils** inside the refrigerator. In these heat-exchanging pipes, the coolant changes from a liquid to a gas. This keeps the air inside the fridge "cold."

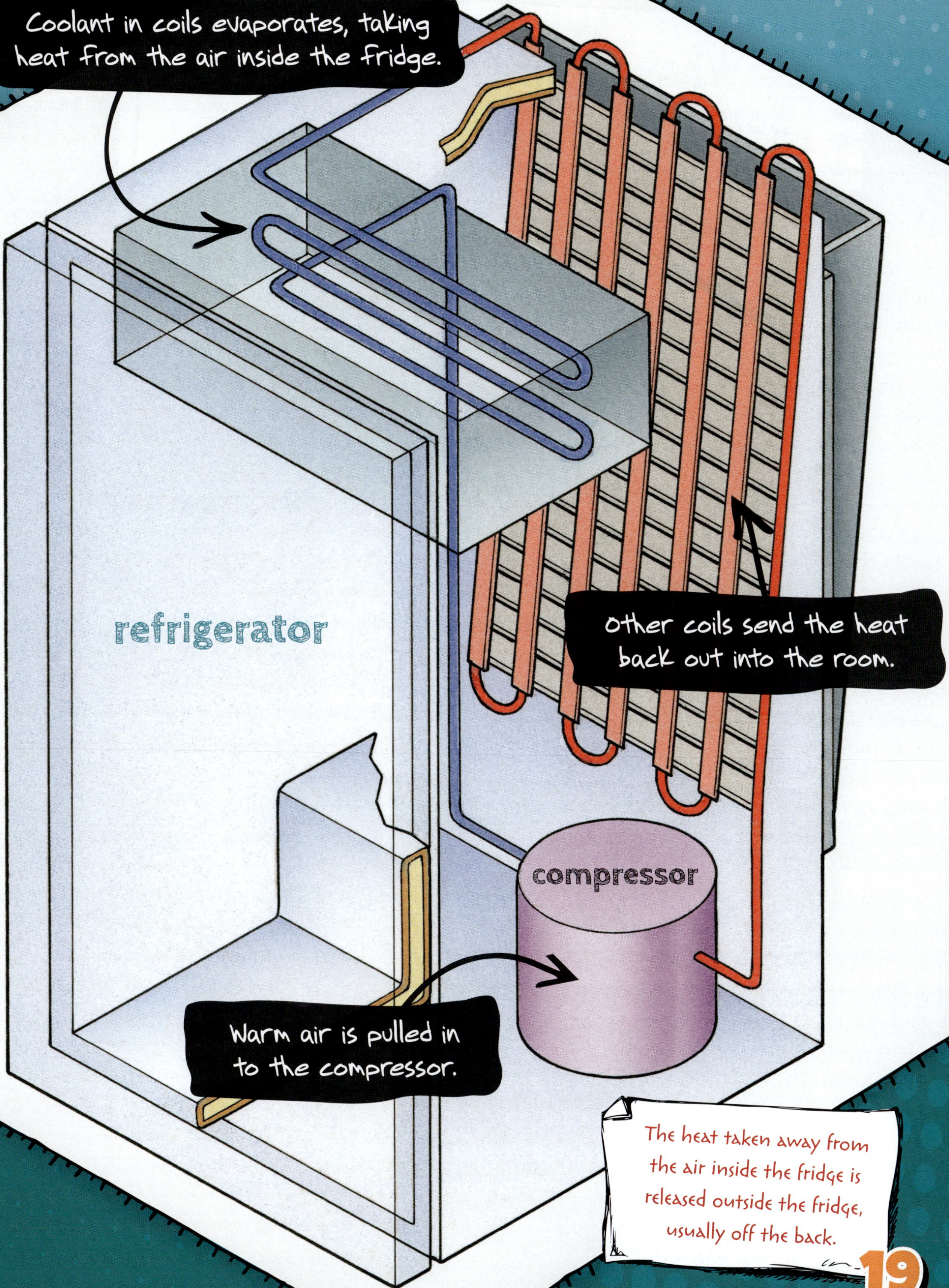

The heat taken away from the air inside the fridge is released outside the fridge, usually off the back.

Q: What makes light bulbs burn out?

A: Inside the glass of an old light bulb, there are two thin wires that are connected by a filament. This filament is what makes the bulb light. Filaments turn electricity into heat and light energy. However, filaments don't last forever. Every time they're turned on, a little bit of the metal gets so hot it evaporates. Eventually, the filament gets too thin and breaks. That's why we say a light bulb "burns out." It actually burns away!

NOT For Long!

The light bulbs that use filaments that burn out are called incandescent light bulbs. In 2007, a law passed with a plan to stop these kinds of light bulbs from being made in the United States because they aren't very energy efficient. The law took effect in 2012. However, many people still use incandescent light bulbs in their homes and businesses. So many were made for so long that supplies are still available.

Cool Light

Some types of lights, such as **fluorescent** lights and **LEDs**, are called "cool lights" because they produce less heat. They need less energy to light up, which means they're more efficient.

Q: Who invented the vacuum?

A: There were many people who played a part in creating the vacuums we use today! In 1869, an inventor named Ives McGaffey created a "sweeping machine." He had the first **patent** for something that could clean rugs, but it didn't have a motor like modern vacuums. In 1899, John Thurman invented a gas-powered vacuum. By 1903, Thurman was taking his horse-drawn vacuum to people's houses! It cost about $4 per visit.

But it was Englishman Hubert Cecil Booth who patented a motorized vacuum cleaner that successfully used **suction** to clean in 1901. His machine would be parked outside a building while hoses were fed through the windows to clean! A smaller vacuum that could be used easily in homes was patented in 1908, and soon William Hoover bought that patent and made the design even better.

Vacuums use a fan to create a vacuum, or a completely empty space, and use suction to pull in air as well as dust and dirt.

Learning the Loop

Q: How can a roller coaster go upside down?

A: Roller coasters are a lot of fun. They can go up, down, and even upside down in a loop-the-loop, all without an engine and always staying on their track!

This is possible because of physics forces. Roller coasters have huge drops at the beginning to get the cars going fast. First, roller coaster cars are pulled up a big hill with a cable or pulley. When the cars get over the top, they start speeding down the hill. At a great enough speed, when they reach a loop, force is applied outward, away from the center of the loop. The cars and the people in them are pressed to the outside of the loop. At the top of the loop, the **acceleration** force is stronger than gravity and is pulling upward. **Inertia** keeps riders in their seats.

Elliptical LOOPS

Loop-the-loops are actually oblong, or somewhat egg shaped. If they were too circular, the force applied would be too strong, and they wouldn't be safe to ride on!

Q: Why don't escalators run out of stairs?

A: Escalators produce step after step, seeming to go on forever. Each stair is connected to a chain that wraps around two gears, one at the top of the escalator and one at the bottom. The chain moves around the gears in a flat circle. Most of this moving chain is hidden beneath the stairs of the escalator in a big metal container, or truss.

Inside an Escalator Truss

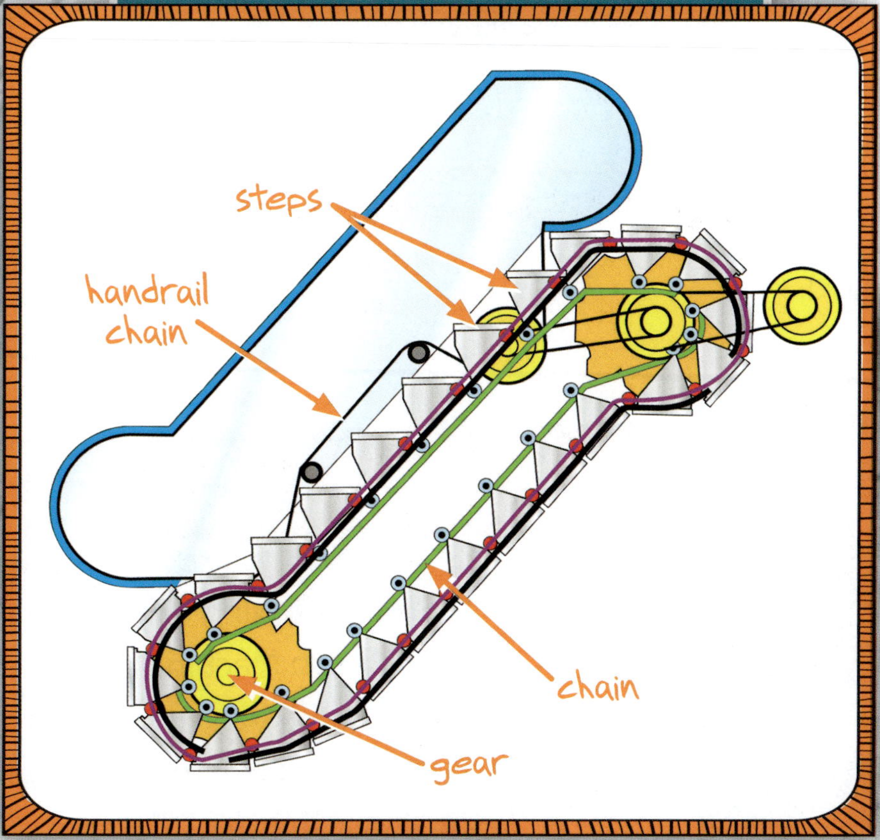

RIGHT Side Up

Each escalator stair has two sets of wheels. The set near the top of the stair is connected to the rotating chain and pulls the stair along. The lower set glides along a track below the chain. When the stairs are ready to come up from the truss, the tracks level out, so that the stairs come up flat and level. Then, when the stair disappears at the top of the escalator, they drop down, and the whole stair flips upside down! Then it rides around the chain to come back up again.

Renewable Energy

Q: How do wind turbines make energy?

A: Wind turbines are a popular way to gather the **renewable** energy of the wind. Like the skateboard, the wind turbine is a simple machine—a wheel and an axle.

Wind turbines have big blades. When a gust of wind blows, it pushes these blades, and they move around in a circle. The blades are connected to a shaft, and the shaft connects to a generator, which uses the energy to make electricity. The more wind, the more the blades turn, the more energy is generated.

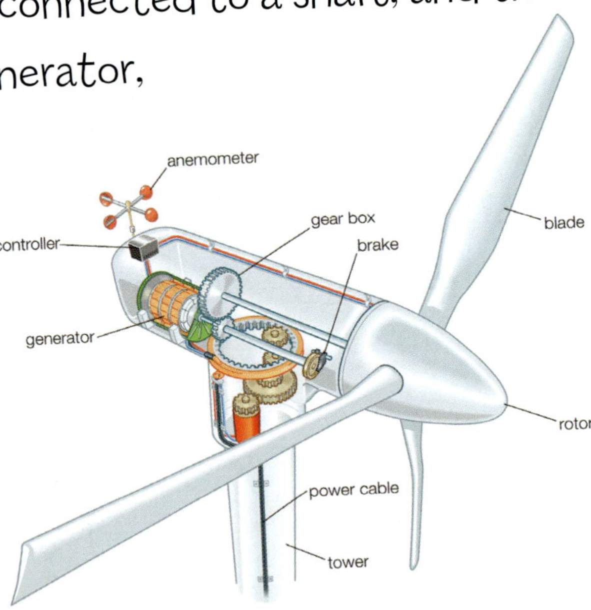

Getting Charged Up

The first electric wind turbine was called the Brush Machine and was invented by Charles F. Brush in 1888. It generated electricity outside Cleveland, Ohio, for 20 years.

Wind turbines are often found on hillsides, near mountains, and by water. Many people are studying how to make wind turbines more efficient.

Glossary

acceleration: the rate at which an object changes its velocity, which is the rate at which an object changes its position

axle: a pin or bar that wheels rotate around

battery: a device that turns chemical energy into electricity

coil: a series of loops

combustion: a process or instance of burning

complex: having to do with something with many parts that work together

conscious: aware, mindful

coolant: a liquid used to cool

deplete: to lessen

drag: a force generated by the movement of a solid object through a fluid or gas that works to slow the forward motion of the solid object

evaporate: to change from a liquid into a gas

fluorescent: having to do with the light created when electricity flows through the gas in a glass tube

friction: the force that slows motion between two objects moving over each other

inertia: a property of matter that says matter remains in motion or at rest unless acted upon by some outside force

LED: a kind of light source called a light emitting diode

levitation: the act of floating in the air

patent: an official document that gives a person the rights to a design, machine, or process for a time. Also, the obtaining of this document.

physics: the study of matter, energy, force, and motion, and the relationship among them

pivot: to move around a center point

renewable: capable of being replaced in natural ecological cycles

suction: the act of sucking in

technology: the practical application of specialized knowledge

For More Information

BOOKS

Arnold, Nick. *How Machines Work: The Interactive Guide to Simple Machines and Mechanisms.* Philadelphia, PA: Running Press Kids, 2011.

Doudna, Kelly. *The Kids' Book of Simple Machines: Cool Projects & Activities That Make Science Fun.* Minneapolis, MN: Mighty Media Kids, 2015.

Walker, Sally M., and Feldmann, Roseann. *Put to the Test: Pulleys.* Minneapolis, MN: Lerner Publications, 2012.

WEBSITES

How Does a Car Engine Work Video for Kids
easyscienceforkids.com/how-does-the-car-engine-work-video-for-kids/
Check out this video to review how cars work.

Simple Machines: Facts
idahoptv.org/sciencetrek/topics/simple_machines/facts.cfm
Learn about each type of simple machine and how it works.

Index